Timmy Tern's
Odyssey

In Search of an Endless Summer

Alex J Bo

Chennai • Bangalore

CLEVER FOX PUBLISHING
Chennai, India

Published by CLEVER FOX PUBLISHING 2023
Copyright © Alex J Bo 2023

All Rights Reserved.
Paperback: 978-93-56485-11-2
Hardback: 978-93-56485-12-9

This book has been published with all reasonable efforts taken to make the material error-free after the consent of the author. No part of this book shall be used, reproduced in any manner whatsoever without written permission from the author, except in the case of brief quotations embodied in critical articles and reviews.

The Author of this book is solely responsible and liable for its content including but not limited to the views, representations, descriptions, statements, information, opinions and references ["Content"]. The Content of this book shall not constitute or be construed or deemed to reflect the opinion or expression of the Publisher or Editor. Neither the Publisher nor Editor endorse or approve the Content of this book or guarantee the reliability, accuracy or completeness of the Content published herein and do not make any representations or warranties of any kind, express or implied, including but not limited to the implied warranties of merchantability, fitness for a particular purpose. The Publisher and Editor shall not be liable whatsoever for any errors, omissions, whether such errors or omissions result from negligence, accident, or any other cause or claims for loss or damages of any kind, including without limitation, indirect or consequential loss or damage arising out of use, inability to use, or about the reliability, accuracy or sufficiency of the information contained in this book.

Illustrated by: Ratheesh Vincent

In the middle of a large colony of eggs and a few newly hatched baby Arctic terns, an egg begins to shake. It slowly cracks from the inside. Voila! Out comes little Timmy. He looks around in amazement as his mom feeds him. He takes his tiny first steps, tumbles over, toddles again. Poor Timmy cannot fly yet. So, he continues to happily explore his nest with his siblings.

A few weeks went by. Timmy has grown up and can now dive into the water to catch fish to feed himself. But, Timmy notices that it has been getting colder with each passing day.

And one fine day, the water freezes and turns to ice. Timmy realizes that he must go to a different place if he has to find food and protect himself from the cold. He is very excited about his first long journey and decides to take off before his family and friends.

Timmy waves his little wings and bids goodbye to his family. He excitedly flaps his wings and takes off from the icy Arctic. He is eager to discover what adventure awaits him on his first long flight as he starts this epic journey from the North Pole to the South Pole.

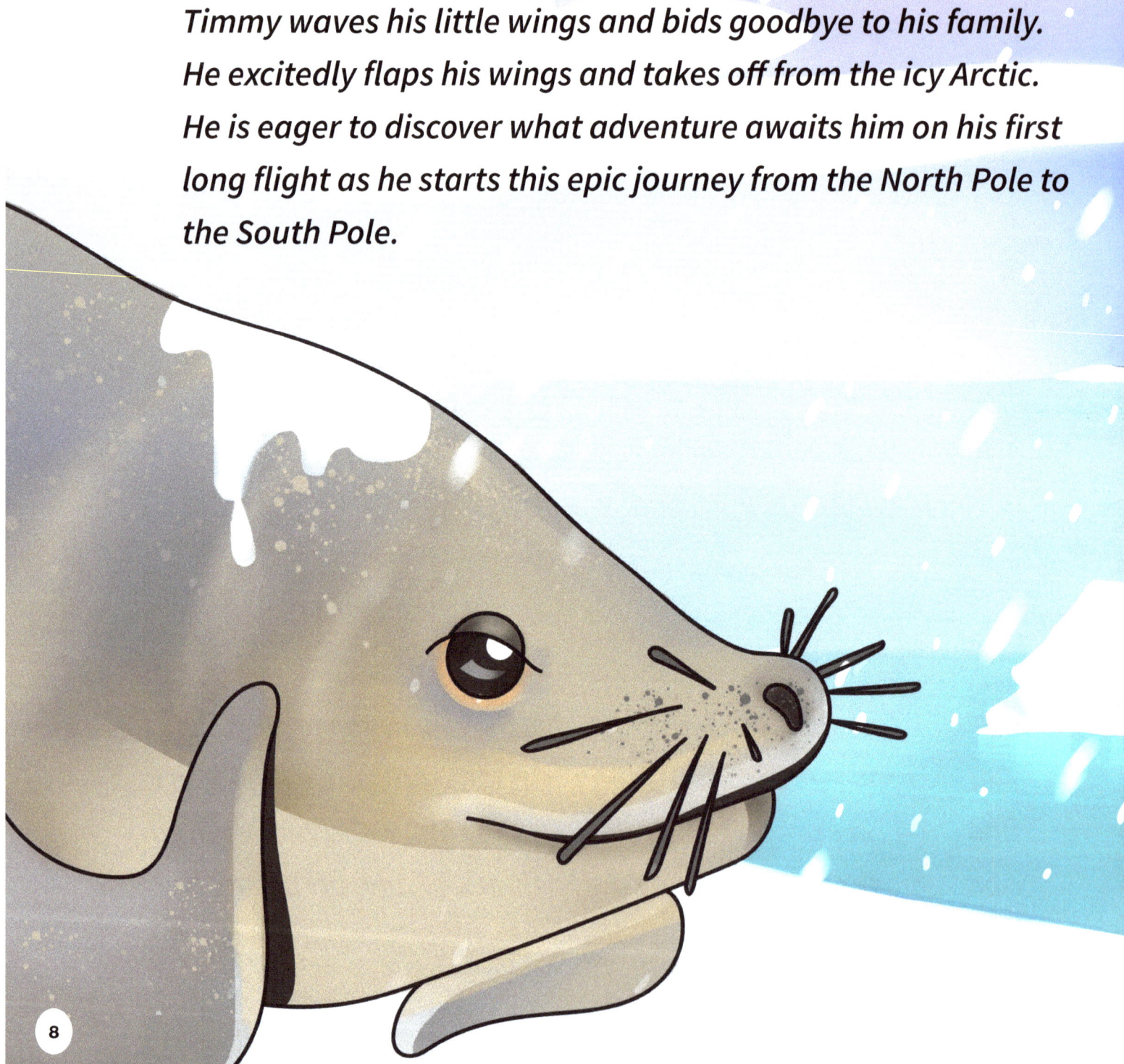

As Timmy flies towards the Antarctic, he glides close to the water in the ocean as the sun shines brightly above him.

Yes! This is what I have been longing for since the start of winter.

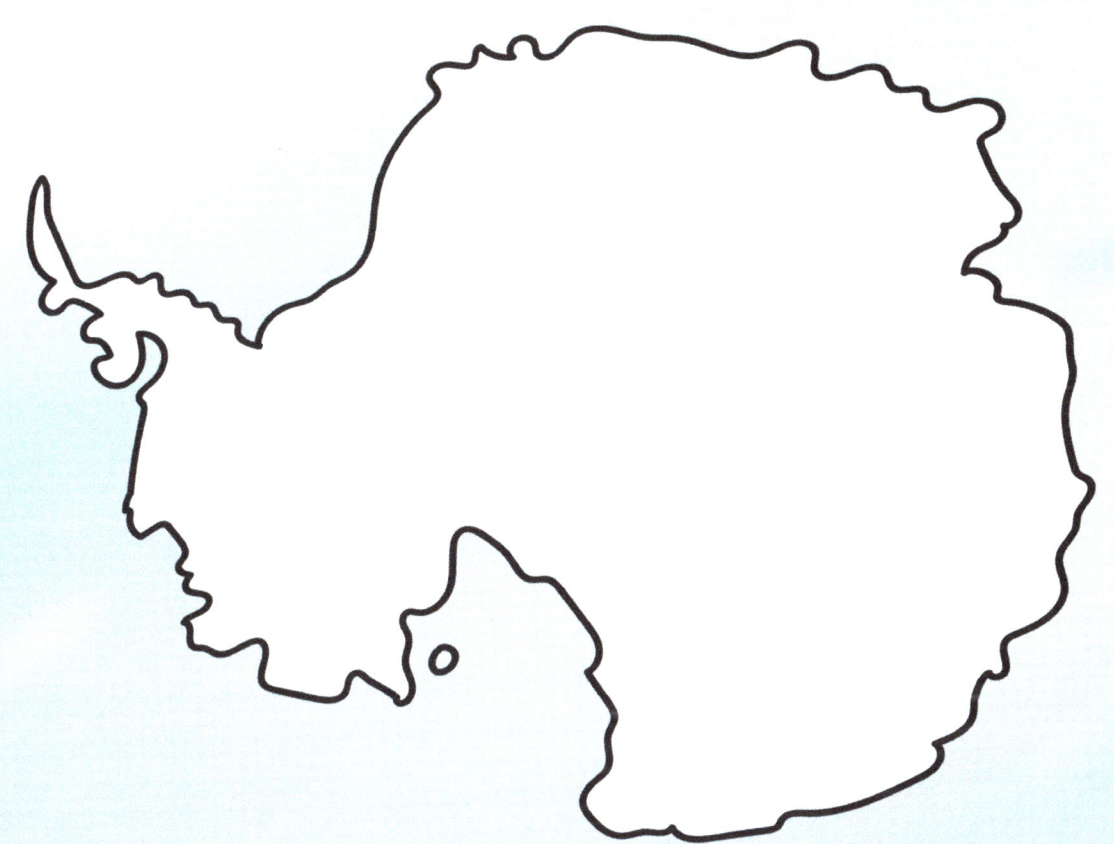

He playfully skims the top of the waves with his wings. Then, in one swift flight, he launches himself back into the air. He swoops down and soars high, feeling sudden bursts of joy. The mighty ocean reflects the sunlight, guiding him towards warmer regions in the south. And the warmth of the sun soothes his wings as he flies through the cold breeze.

As Timmy continues to fly, far off on the horizon, he sees a piece of land amidst the seemingly endless stretch of water.

That has to be Patagonia for sure.

As he approaches the land, he is awed by the sight of snowy white peaks, glittery blue lakes, and lush green forests. He decides to explore this picturesque landscape before continuing his journey.

Timmy swiftly glides through the sky and swoops down close to the land of Patagonia.

*A herd of deer catches
Timmy's attention
as he hovers above
Patagonia's forests.
As he admires them,
a playful fox running
around the shrubs of the
low mountains dazzles and
amuses Timmy.*

At the southern end of South America, shared by the countries of Argentina and Chile, lies a vast region of wilderness and natural beauty called Patagonia.

Nearby, Timmy also notices an Andean Condor – a giant black vulture with greyish white wings and neck feathers.

Patagonia has unique plants and animals that can be found only here. This unique combination of plants and animals along with their surroundings forms a "bubble of life" called the ecosystem. Deer, Andean condors, Magellanic penguins, gray foxes, and many more species live together in Patagonia.

Some Sanderling families have also come to Patagonia to escape the freezing temperatures of the north. Timmy befriends the Sanderlings just as we make friends with others during our journeys.

Birds like Timmy travel thousands of miles each year in search of food and warmer climates. This annual journey, known as migration, is an important part of their life cycle. Therefore, birds like Timmy who take on such journeys are called migratory birds.

Sanderlings too are migratory birds. They travel long distances from their nesting grounds to their wintering grounds in southern regions like Patagonia, which are warmer.

Timmy and his Sanderling friends fly around the Patagonian desert exploring the landscape.

They glide with the breeze around the icy mountain tops and the dips between the peaks.

They swoop down close to the water in the lakes…

...and hop around the glaciers.

One day, while playing with his friends, Timmy notices that the sky is turning dark and spooky.

Rain and storms are approaching. It will be a time of distress for all of them. I should act fast to overcome the looming danger.

He and his friends hear frightened cries of the deer, penguins, foxes, and other animals.

Timmy gathers all his friends, and they together start building a shelter to protect themselves from the rain and storms. Like how "little drops of water make the mighty ocean," the work of each animal put together builds a strong protective shelter for Timmy and all his friends.

All the animals huddle together in the shelter they built. They can hear the roaring waves crashing against the rocks outside.
The animals are scared, but they have faith in the shelter that they built together and patiently waited for the storm to pass.

To distract themselves from the frightening sound of the storm outside, they engage in a conversation.

Timmy learns about the different types of penguins and the importance of protecting the ecosystem.

As the conversation continues, Timmy also learns about the negative effects of human activities on the environment and how endangered species like Andean condor and deer need our help to survive.

Meanwhile, the storm passes. All the animals came out of the shelter relieved. However, they are saddened to find out that their homes were damaged by the storm.

All the animals once again team up to clean the mess and rebuild their damaged homes.

Timmy is filled with joy to see the sun shining and the place being rebuilt and coming back to life again.

Timmy realizes that it is time to continue his migratory journey further south. He waves his wings and bids goodbye to all his friends and promises to visit them every year during winter.

Timmy smiles and cherishes the memories of his friends as he flaps and takes off towards Antarctica. Thinking back on how he and his friends overcame the crisis, Timmy understands the importance of teamwork and coordination.

Although Timmy is sad about leaving his friends in Patagonia, he knows that they will continue being friends even if they do not meet for a long time. He understands that he has to continue heading southwards to complete his migration. Timmy looks forward to making new friends and is excited about what lies ahead in this epic adventure.

www.ingramcontent.com/pod-product-compliance
Lightning Source LLC
LaVergne TN
LVHW070535070526
838199LV00075B/6780